St. Ivo And The Ashes: A Correct, True And Particular History Of Ivo Bligh's Crusade In Australia

R. D. Beeston

In the interest of creating a more extensive selection of rare historical book reprints, we have chosen to reproduce this title even though it may possibly have occasional imperfections such as missing and blurred pages, missing text, poor pictures, markings, dark backgrounds and other reproduction issues beyond our control. Because this work is culturally important, we have made it available as a part of our commitment to protecting, preserving and promoting the world's literature. Thank you for your understanding.

St. Ivo & the Ashes

A

CORRECT, TRUE & PARTICULAR HISTORY

OF THE

HON. IVO BLIGH'S CRUSADE IN AUSTRALIA.

BY

R. D. BEESTON.

ILLUSTRATED BY

M. C. B. MASSIE.

1882-3.

Melbourne:
AUSTRALIAN PRESS AGENCY.
ALBERT S. MANDERS & CO., 91 LITTLE COLLINS STREET EAST.

PREFACE.

In submitting this little *brochure* to the consideration of that portion of the English and Australian public who take an interest in cricket, we would ask for a kind reception and not a close criticism.

The sketches are the *facta similia* (though reduced by the kind aid of Mr. Noone, of the Survey Department, under the photolithographic process) of a series of pen and ink sketches made during the progress of the matches in Australia. They excited considerable interest at the time, and it occurred to the artist and the author—then visiting in Melbourne, that the series, accompanied by a humorous but a correct description, would find a favorable reception among cricketers throughout the British Empire.

To our friends in the colonies and to such of our old comrades as may be in any part of the Queen's Dominions we dedicate our little venture.

       M. C. B. MASSIE,
         Late 13th Light Dragoons.

       R. D. BEESTON,
         Late Bengal Staff Corps.

St. Ivo and the Ashes.

TOWARDS the close of the English Cricket Season of 1882, the Australian Eleven, under the captaincy of Mr. W. L. Murdoch, "put a set" on home cricketers, and created dismay in English cricketing circles by defeating the "Gentlemen of England," a picked team of whom had a crushing dose of gruel administered to them at the Kennington Oval. With 33 runs only to get to win, seven of the best bats in England failed to score more than 26, leaving the Australians winners by seven runs.

The *London Sportsman* took a gloomy (not to say funereal) view of the affair, and in its columns, subsequently, published an *In Memoriam* "to the ashes of English cricket, which found their last resting-place on Kennington Oval." The *Sportsman's* idea evidently was that there was no more "cricket on the (H)earth," as far as England was concerned, and the loss of the *(H)ashes* put the staff into various *stews*.

The Australian Cricket Season saw the arrival in the antipodes of the Hon. Ivo Bligh and his team, who have since won such golden opinions from all classes in all the colonies they visited during their tour.

In replying to the toast of "The English Team," on his arrival in Melbourne, Mr. Bligh humorously declared that he and his eleven had come to "beard the kangaroo in his den, and try to recover *those* ashes." How far he succeeded in the attempt the accompanying sketches will, it is hoped, fairly and impartially show.

It is not my intention, in this little *brochure*, to go into the question as to whether the English team was or was not the best that could have been got together. Whether the inclusion of Ulyett, Lucas, Grace, and Hornby would have been more conducive to the success of the "ashes" expedition, is beside the question. The fact remains that the team, as was fully proved, was an uncommonly good one, including first-class exponents of every department of the game; and in spite of the absence from their ranks of the great W. G., they managed to *ingraciate* themselves with all colonists with whom they came in contact.

The First and Second Contests.

The first of the three tussels with Murdoch's Eleven resulted in an undeniable defeat for the crusaders; the Lion was hopped round so skilfully by the agile marsupial that the latter scored a win by nine wickets.

St. Ivo and his knights, no doubt considering a change of air would be beneficial, then took a tour in Tasmania, beating a Northern and Southern Eighteen in the "tight little island," and returned to Victoria like giants refreshed to once more grapple with Captain Murdoch and his victorious followers.

Whether it was owing to the Tasmanian climate, the bright eyes of the Insular ladies (unsurpassed in any portion of the globe), the extreme soundness of the beer brewed in the locality, or all three causes combined, deponent sayeth not; but it is certain that on January 19th, 20th, and 22nd the seekers after the "ashes" were all in tip-top form—full of pluck, confidence, and determination, each man to do his level best. Add to this that the spectators were thoroughly impartial in their applause, the lion coming in for as good a share as the whelps; and it will be seen the only other adjacent to real good sport was the kind consideration of the "clerk of the weather."

It must be confessed, however, that this meteorological functionary—like Mrs. Prig in discussing the contents of Mrs. Gamp's teapot—did not quite "act fair."

St. Ivo's lucky shilling (or copper) won the toss, and the crusaders went to bat on a grand wicket, in grand weather, encouraged by the presence of a a grand assemblage of spectators.

Barlow, the Lancashire stonewaller, partnered by the crack Cambridge bat, C. T. Studd, led off; and to show there was no desire on either of their parts to outstrip the other, each made 14, and each also obligingly condescended to let Palmer take their wickets—not the first occasion on record, by the way, where Crusaders have been euchred by a Palmer. Leslie and Steel, the dark blue and the light, held their ground most stubbornly, threes coming to the former as easily as though he were a second Euclid busily engaged in manufacturing triangles, while Steel, whose preference for *singles* would seem to show he is not a marrying man, would occasionally go in for *double* blessedness by cutting a two, and drove one four which was not "in hand" of any fieldsman. The light blue at length succumbed to M'Donnell, who held a catch which was *Giffen* off the South Australian trundler; and Leslie, after running up a score of 54, finished by running up himself to the wicket just too late. It is said that "he who runs may read," a proverb, the monotony of which was varied on this occasion by the Surrey crack, who clearly demonstrated that "he who is Read may run," which he did most effectually to the tune of 75, Palmer eventually *palming* a catch off his own bowling. Barnes, apparently, was not the representative of noughts (Notts) on this occasion, for he insisted on compiling 32 before

Nº 1 Plate.

THE KANGAROO SCORES FIRST
Australians by 9 Wickets.
30 Decr 1882. 1–2 Jany 1883
Melbourne

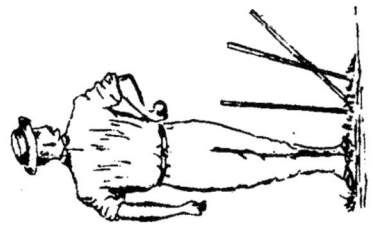

his wicket was *Giffen* away to become the property of the South Australian. Then the game bore the appearance for a short time of being played on the *Oval*, for St. Ivo and Tylecote succeeded in hatching each a duck. The Yorkshire tyke, however, showed his objection to an omelette diet by speedily smashing *his* egg, and made a will ere his demise, on which the personalty was over the half-hundred, the scoring-board showing 55 *pro Bates*. (N.B.—This requires thinking over, but it will amply repay perusal.) The initials of the younger Studd must have signified Go Back on this occasion, as he soon retired to the pavilion clean bowled for 1, without letting Morley get his mawleys on the ball. The sundries amounted to 10 (got in divers ways), and the total of the innings reached the formidable number of 294.

Palmer and Giffen "scooped the pool" in bowling honours, the Victorian getting five wickets, and the Adelaide man four. Blackham Murdoch, and Giffen shared the honours of missing Read, one miss to each being on record; and Barnes should have been run out, but he wasn't, but got two extra runs *in* instead. "Infelix," in the *Australasian*, naively remarked that "the worst feature about the fielding of our men was their inability to hold the catches." Well, this may be a Felix or Infelix remark, but you can bet odds any day that the "inability to hold the catches" is undoubtedly the *very* "worst feature" of a fieldsman.

Those two Sydney cracks, Massie and Bannerman, first wielded the willow for Australia, the former retiring—bowled by Barlow—only when 43 had been *amassied* to his credit. The stonewaller "held the fort" for a long time against all comers, till a ball from the Yorkshireman, Bates, downed his defence, and he followed H. H. M. to the pavilion. Murdoch filled the gap, with Horan, the captain evidently bent on taking up a permanent residence at the wicket. Not so the Jolimonter; he retired, caught by the Yorkshire tyke off his own bowling, for 3. Giffen arrived on the scene, only to receive his quietus from the inexorable North County trundler, while the giant Bonner—just to vary the last comer's luck—obligingly got caught off his first ball, instead of bowled. Bates thereby did the "hat trick"; and the score of the Australians began to look as blank as their faces. Barnes, not wishing all the bowling honours to fall to Bates, kindly dismissed Blackham for 5; and the irrepressible Yorkshireman clean bowled the next three men—Garrett (for 10), Palmer (for 7), and Spofforth, for that article of hen manufacture which is so acceptable on a well-ordered breakfast-table, provided it is like Cæsar's wife—above suspicion. Murdoch, the dauntless, carried out his bat for 19, and the innings closed for 114, Bates securing seven wickets for 28 runs. Murdoch stopped at the wickets two hours and more for his 19, giving two very hard chances—one to Tylecote, and one to Steel—neither of which were accepted. During the Australian innings the "clerk of the weather" behaved badly, the light being very bad; and the Antipodean batsmen got the same favor from him in their second attempt. With 180 behind, Murdoch and Bannerman went to the wickets with the forlorn hope of saving a one innings defeat. That horrid Yorkshireman, however, was about again, and got the Australian captain for 17, clean bowling him with a "caution," while the little stonewaller put a ball into Ivo's hands at point. "*I vowed* I'd hold it" said the English captain, as Alick went back to the pavilion on urgent private affairs. Blackham scored 6, and was clean bowled by Barlow, who was evidently jealous of the honour of Lancashire in the trundling department. Bonner hit hard and straight, and played good cricket, retiring at length for 34, caught by Morley off Barlow, Horan being caught by the same fieldsman off Bates for 15. The Yorkshire crack clean bowled M'Donnell for 13; and it was pretty evident that in this match at least those "ashes" were not so firmly planted in Australian soil. Massie, after scoring 10, fell a victim to Barlow, being well caught by C. T. Studd, and joined the melancholy prosession to the paviiion. Ivo caught Giffen off Bates for 19, and Barnes secured Garrett off the same bowler for 6. G. B. Studd made a splendid catch off Bates' bowling, thereby sending Palmer to the right-about with 4, and upsetting Spofforth's apple-cart, who retired not out 14—three 4's and a double. Total of innings, 153, the "ashes' being recovered by the infliction on the Australians of a one innings defeat, and 27 runs to spare. Australia, despondent; England, radiantly jubilant, and great enthusiasm all round. Ivo and his comrades were called to the front, and enthusiastically cheered. The two captains made speeches of condolence and congratulation. Champagne flowed, and everything was jolly and "up to the knocker." Murdoch congratulated the winners, and hoped the result would be reversed in Sydney. If Ivo hoped so too, he did not express himself to that effect, and the rival teams went home to dinner.

The Convincing Match.

The Lion and the agile Kangaroo were now "one all" in the fight for the "ashes," the former more eager than ever to follow up his victory; the latter on his mettle to avert a second defeat. Both sides determined to do their level best, and both carried out their determination. It was as far as merits went—six of one, and half-a-dozen of the other—when lo! that mysteriously disposed "clerk of the weather" went over to the Englishmen, and put his casting vote in their favour.

That lucky coin of St. Ivo's proved its utility once more, and the crusaders went first to the wickets, which were in splendid condition, the weather everything that could be desired, and the light just suited for scoring.

C. T. Studd and Barlow, as usual, showed the way, the former studying the bowling to such good purpose that he soon compiled 21, when Blackham caught him off Garrett. Barlow put together 28 for the honour of Lancashire, and then obligingly hit Spofforth into Murdoch's tenacious grip, and followed the Cantab crack to the pavilion. Leslie, the tower of batting strength of the eleven, went sorrowfully in the same direction a disappointed conchologist, with a shell—an egg shell—

his possession, which he had failed to crack. Steel made (or *stole*) 7, when one of Garrett's "so softly o'er him *stealing*," relegated him to seclusion and *reverie*. Barnes was sacrificed for 2, Blackham catching him off Spofforth. Now came the stand. Read and Tylecote got together, and looked as though the partnership was going to be a "lifer." Every bowler was tried in succession, but only with the result of a quickly increasing score. Between them they made 132 runs, each tying for 66. Read was caught by Massie off Bannerman, and the English wicket-keeper was run out. The Yorkshire bowler made 19, when he was caught by M'Donnell off Spofforth. G. B. Studd scored 3, and was clean bowled by Palmer, who performed the same kind office by the English captain, after the latter had scored 13. Morley carried his bat out for 2, and the first innings of the crusaders closed for the capital total of 247.

During the night "Jupiter Pluvius" made matters lively by drenching the wickets thoroughly, and the morning of the second day dawned bleak and dismal. The hopes of Australian sympathisers, like the wickets, were considerably damped; and the clouds looked as black as their chances. However, "faint heart never dried a wet cricket ground," so Giffen, accompanied by little Bannerman, strode to their posts, determined to "do or die." Little Alick felt that "Australia this day expected every man to do his duty," and, for once in his life, opened his shoulders, and hit as vigorously as Bonnor himself, causing the crusaders to expand their under lips pretty considerably. Giffen, too, played slashing cricket, and when the latter was disposed of—by a smart piece of stumping by Tylecote—76 runs had been totalled, of which the South Australian had scored 41. Captain Murdoch now joined Bannerman, but did not seem to like the bowling at all. Just after the century appeared on the board, the elements combined to sluice all the players back to the pavilion, whence they did not emerge until past five o'clock. When the stumps were drawn for the day, Australia had lost one wicket for 133 runs, Bannerman being not out, with 68 to his credit. This performance, on such a sodden wicket, was a truly memorable one; and the plucky little batsman was warmly applauded. All Saturday night, and all Sunday the rain came down; and, by the appearance of the weather, it seemed probable that the match would have to be played out in canoes. Monday, however, dawned bright and fine, the wicket being soft and spongy. Murdoch left the partnership first, being given out leg before wicket to Steel. M'Donnell, who succeeded, was clean bowled by the Cantab for a "duck's egg," and Horan filled the gap. Bannerman's time came next, he being caught by Bates off Morley, and retired with 94 to his credit, amidst a storm of applause, in which the Englishmen heartily joined. Massie came—and went, caught splendidly at point by the English captain, after scoring a single. Bonnor was magnificently caught by G. B. Studd off Morley, without adding to the score, 6—0—173; and the Lion rustled his mane, while the Kangaroo walked round with subdued tail. Horan next retired, caught by Steel off Morley, for 19. Garrett came in, and, accepting a "duck's egg," retired. Palmer and Blackham then fetched the score to 210, when the former was caught by G. B. Studd off Barnes, and vanished with 7 to his credit. Spofforth arrived in time to see Blackham clean bowled by Barlow, for a well played 27 ; and the Australian innings closed for 218, or 29 behind the crusaders.

Leslie and C. T. Studd started the second innings of the Englishmen, the latter scoring 8, and the former 25. The ground was too sticky for heavy scoring; the only other double figures in this innings being Barlow 24, Read 21, and Captain Ivo (not out) 17, the total score being 123.

On the morning of the fourth day, with 153 to get to win, a hot sun glowing overhead, and a "baked" wicket, Giffen and Bannerman led the van. Giffen was bowled for 11, and the stonewaller well caught at point for 5. Murdoch was caught for a "duck's egg," and the "ashes" floated loosely on Australian soil. Then Horan was run out for 8, and Massie caught for 11. Six wickets for 33 runs; and "all Lombard-street to a China orange" that the "ashes" were recovered. Blackham and Bonner pulled the score up to 56, when Barlow scattered the "giant's" timbers. Spofforth filled the gap, and, with the score at 72, put one into Steel's hands, and sought the inner recesses of the pavilion. Barlow next bowled Blackham for 26, and Garrett for a "duck's egg," Palmer carrying his bat out for 2 ; and the match was over, won by the Englishmen by 69 runs.

The Englishmen tugged the longest, and the Lion, harnessed to a car containing the sacred ashes, galloped gaily in the direction of his native country.

Ivo Bligh's Eleven v. Combined Australia.

So the battle for the "ashes" was over, and once more the Englishmen had regained their lost supremacy in the cricket field. Neither Lion nor Kangaroo, however, was satisfied, apparently. The latter considered he had been unfairly dealt with by the "clerk of the weather ;" and the former, in the elation of his victory, "offered one more chance" against a more representative Australian Eleven. Massie, M'Donnell, and Garrett gave place to Midwinter, Evans, and Boyle ; and the dates fixed for the "one more chance" to come off were February 17th., 19th., and 20th., and the place the Association Ground at Sydney.

Again that lucky coin of the English captain's turned up "trumps," and the crusaders went first to the wickets, C. T. Studd and Barlow being the pioneers of the team. Midwinter secured the latter's wicket he being caught by Murdoch at point after scoring 2. Leslie joined Studd, and the rival University representatives both began run-getting at a fair rate, until the Oxford man was caught in the slips by Bonnor off Boyle, and retired for 17. Steel joined Studd, and the partnership was not dissolved until 110 appeared on the board, when Studd was run out for a fine innings of 48. Read arrived on the scene, and left shortly after, being caught by Bonnor off Boyle, after scoring 11. Tylecote came, and was clean bowled by Boyle for 5 ; and Barnes quickly retired, dismissed by a "corker" from the "demon," having only added 2 to the score. Bates added 9, and was magnificently caught by Bonnor.

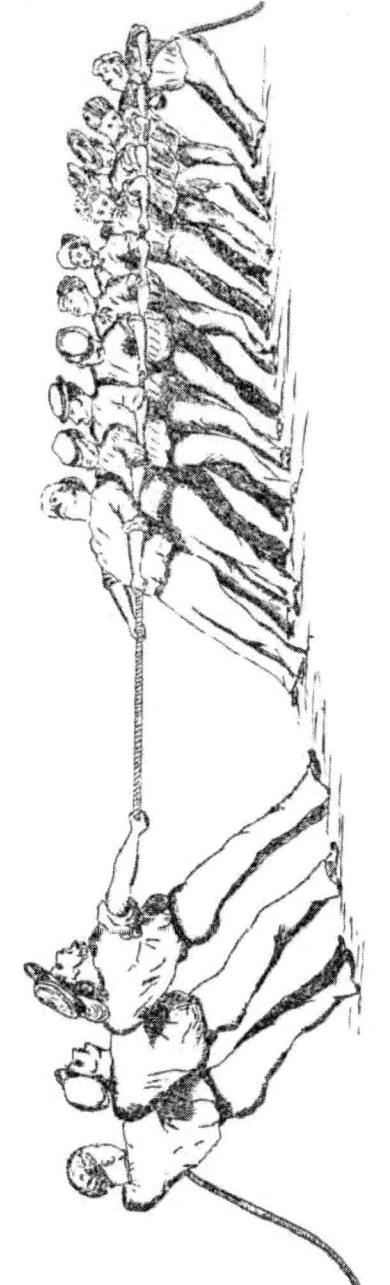

THE ASHES GONE

IVO! NO! IVO!

Then forth strode the captain, amid a storm of applause. He put on 19, when Palmer bowled him with a leg break. G. B. Studd took his place; Steel all this while scoring as though batting was his own invention. Studd, after scoring 3, was run out, and the stumps drawn for the day. On resuming on the second day, Morley was clean bowled by Palmer without scoring, and the innings closed for 263, Steel carrying out his bat for the grand score of 135.

Bonnor and Bannerman—the long and the short of it—led off for the Australians. After scoring 10 the "little un" had to go, caught by Barlow off Morley; and Murdoch, who took his place, was clean bowled by the Lancashire professional for the—by no means coveted—egg. Horan came, scored 4, and retired, caught by G. B. Studd off Morley. Giffen, who was lame, came to the crease, having Murdoch to run for him. After scoring 27, the Adelaide man was caught by the ubiquitous G. B. Studd. Meanwhile Bonnor had been scoring rapidly, and missed repeatedly, Steel, Barlow, and Read having each let him off; and the board showed 4—27—113. Midwinter was clean bowled by Barlow, after scoring 10. Blackham joined Bonnor, and between them the score rose to 160, when the "giant" was at length caught by Barlow, after scoring 87. Palmer retired for nothing, caught by Bligh off Steel; and Evans arrived. Blackham was at length clean bowled by Bates for 57, and Boyle and Evans carried the score up to 248, when the stumps were drawn. Boyle was caught by G. B. Studd off Barlow on the third day, and the Australians' innings closed for 262; Evans (not out), 22, the total being just one short of the English score.

Limited space forbids dwelling too long on the second innings of the two teams. Bates made top score for the crusaders, with 48 (not out); O. T. Studd, 31; Steel, 21; Barlow and Barnes, 20 a-piece, and Leslie, 19. The innings closed for 197, leaving the Australians 199 to get to win.

The Australians' second innings commenced in anything but a propitious manner, their first three wickets (Murdoch, Bonnor, and Horan) falling for 51. Giffen and Bannerman, however, got together, and brought the score up to 107, when the latter was caught by Bligh at point, after putting together 63 in a masterly manner. Blackham, the indomitable, then joined Giffen, and when the latter was stumped by Tylecote, the board showed 5—32—162. Evans joined Blackham, but was caught by Leslie off Steel for 0. Midwinter came to the Victorian wicket-keeper's assistance, the winning hit being made by the latter within a few minutes of time being called, Australia winning by four wickets, amid tremendous cheering.

Once more the "ashes," like Mahomet's coffin, were neither in one place nor the other. The Lion, in full career, broke his harness, and the cart was upset. It remained for Victoria to show where their final resting-place should be fixed

And the joy was great in the Marsupial Camp. The father of all the Kangaroos stood on his head, while the family turned various summersaults.

A learned graduate, who was on the ground, became inspired. Speaking in the ancient Latin tongue, he exclaimed—

Qualia prospiciens, catulus ferit æthera risu,
Ipsaque trans lunæ cornua vacca salit.

Victoria Victrix.

Contrary to general expectation the match in Sydney proved to be the last played between the Englishmen and a representative Australian Eleven. The general wish was to play a return match in Melbourne, but owing to various causes it could not be brought about. Victoria, however, was all there, and the crusaders wound out their campaign by playing Eleven of Victoria. Six of the original Australian Eleven took part in the play, the "new blood" being supplied by Scott, Midwinter, Turner, M'Shane and Cooper. W. H. Cooper captained the team, and handled his forces so well that I can only say this—If our volunteer officers handled *their* men half as well we might perhaps *see* some of that "superior intelligence" we *hear* so much about.

Friday, the 9th day of March, in the year 1883, saw the start of the match. St. Ivo and his lucky coin had evidently fallen out, for the English captain lost the toss, and Victoria went to the wickets.

Percy M'Donnell and swarthy Blackham led the way. The great keeper of the Australian sticks scored a single and was run out, Bonnor taking his place. The giant soon lost Percy, who was caught by Bates off Barnes. Then Scott joined the "big un," and soon made things lively. Scott played a capital innings for 29, when he was smartly caught at the wickets by Tylecote off Barlow. Tommy Horan ran up 37 before he was bowled by Barnes. The "giant" rattled up 54, and was caught at the wickets by the ubiquitous Tylecote. Midwinter played all through the innings, and carried out his bat for 92, great regret being expressed that he had not the chance of reaching three figures. M'Shane justified his selection by making 27, and Turner put 18 together in an artistic manner. Palmer, Boyle and Cooper made respectively 3, 4 and 1, and the innings closed for 284. Victorians jubilant.

Then ensued the most astounding event of the whole of the tour. C. T. Studd and Tylecote went to the wickets to the bowling of W. H. Cooper and Palmer. Tylecote made a pretty cut for 3, and then found to his astonishment that Cooper had bowled him. The insinuating Victorian captain had given his ball instructions to make a flank movement, and, though apparently first wide to leg, it changed front rapidly from the pitch, and caused panic in Tylecote's timber yard. 1—4—5 was the record; English sympathisers astounded, and Victorians as cocky as possible. Bates, the sturdy Yorkshireman, went on only to be clean bowled by a Yorker from Palmer, and the doughty Leslie succumbed, leg before wicket, to the same bowler, also for a "duck." Steel succeeded, and soon put 11 together, when the wriggling Cooper went round him like his namesake round the cask, and found a way to his wicket, 4—11—25, and the best of the English wickets down—bar one. W. W. Read was caught by Midwinter off Cooper for 7. Studd was shortly after bowled by Cooper for 11, and Barlow and Barnes got together. Barnes soon put 11 together, and then Barlow ran him out. 7—11—42, and the elements showed their grief by coming down so heavily that play was stopped for the day. On the last day of the match the wicket was bad and the weather sulky, the result being that the whole of the English team were out for 55. They followed on, and, playing on a horrible wicket, managed to put together 156, Steel contributing 76 by slashing cricket; Barlow 27, and Bates 21 Victoria won the match in one innings and 73 runs to spare.

The lion, slightly dejected and greatly disappointed, lay down, "beaten, but by no means disgraced."

In the dead of night, in a secluded corner of the M.C.C. ground, the lion mournfully buried the ashes, a few kangaroos looking sympathisingly on. The head-stone of the tomb is shaped from a broken bat, on which is the following inscription:

Ci Git

The Sacred Ashes,

awaiting

for a time

The Regaining of Supremacy

by

English Cricket.

N.B.—None of Murdoch's Eleven need apply.

Then the crusaders turned homewards, the lion loth to depart, dragging at his chain as though he would fain try conclusions with the marsupial once again. On the strand the lion regards intently a broken bat. "What will they say in England?" he asks with a sigh, and then reluctantly embarks.

The crusade is over. The ashes are the property of—— aye, there's the rub. Who owns them? Not Murdoch's men They are out of it. Equally clear the crusaders have not made out *their* title. If the property of anyone, I fancy that Victoria should in equity be allowed to hold them for the present.

> Ivo Bligh, you well did try,
>   You'd two successful nicks;
> Now it's done,
> Victoria's won,
>   Got the two odd tricks.
> Hi, Ivo! Ho, Ivo!
>   Speed the parting guest;
> Australians tell you did right well,
>   Tried your level best.
>
> Ivo Bligh, Murdoch's eye
>   Is fairly out of joint;
> You 'gainst W. L.
> Did really well,
>   And fairly scored a point.
> Hi, Ivo! Ho, Ivo! the ashes linger still;
>   Who the urn
>   Will overturn
> Depends on future skill.

BATTING AND BOWLING AVERAGES.

The following *resumé* of of the whole work of the team, from start to finish, including all matches, is from the *Australasian*:—

BATTING AVERAGES IN MATCHES ELEVEN A SIDE.

Batsman's Name.	Matches.	Innings.	Not Out.	Most in an Innings.	Most in a Match.	Total Runs.	Average.
A. G. Steel	7	11	1	*135	156	415	41·5
C. F. H. Leslie	7	11	1	144	144	310	31·0
Barlow	7	12	2	80	80	291	28·1
Bates	7	11	1	*48	57	271	27·1
W. W. Read	7	11	0	75	87	291	26·5
C. T. Studd	7	11	0	56	79	253	28·0
E. F. S. Tylecote	7	11	0	66	71	209	19·0
G. F. Vernon	4	6	1	24	24	60	12·0
Barnes	7	11	1	32	32	113	11·3
Hon. Ivo Bligh	5	9	1	19	30	64	8·0
G. B. Studd	7	12	2	9	12	40	4·0
Morley	5	7	3	3	3	9	2·1

*Signifies not out.

BOWLING AVERAGES IN MATCHES ELEVEN A SIDE.

Bowler's Name.	Balls.	Runs.	Maidens.	Wickets.	Average.
C. F. H. Leslie	172	61	19	4	15·1
A. G. Steel	1134	401	113	25	16·1
W. W. Read	202	91	18	5	18·1
C. T. Studd	778	174	118	9	19·3
Bates	1284	429	150	21	20·9
Barlow	1504	473	203	23	20·13
Morley	748	197	105	8	24·5
Barnes	798	306	75	12	25·6

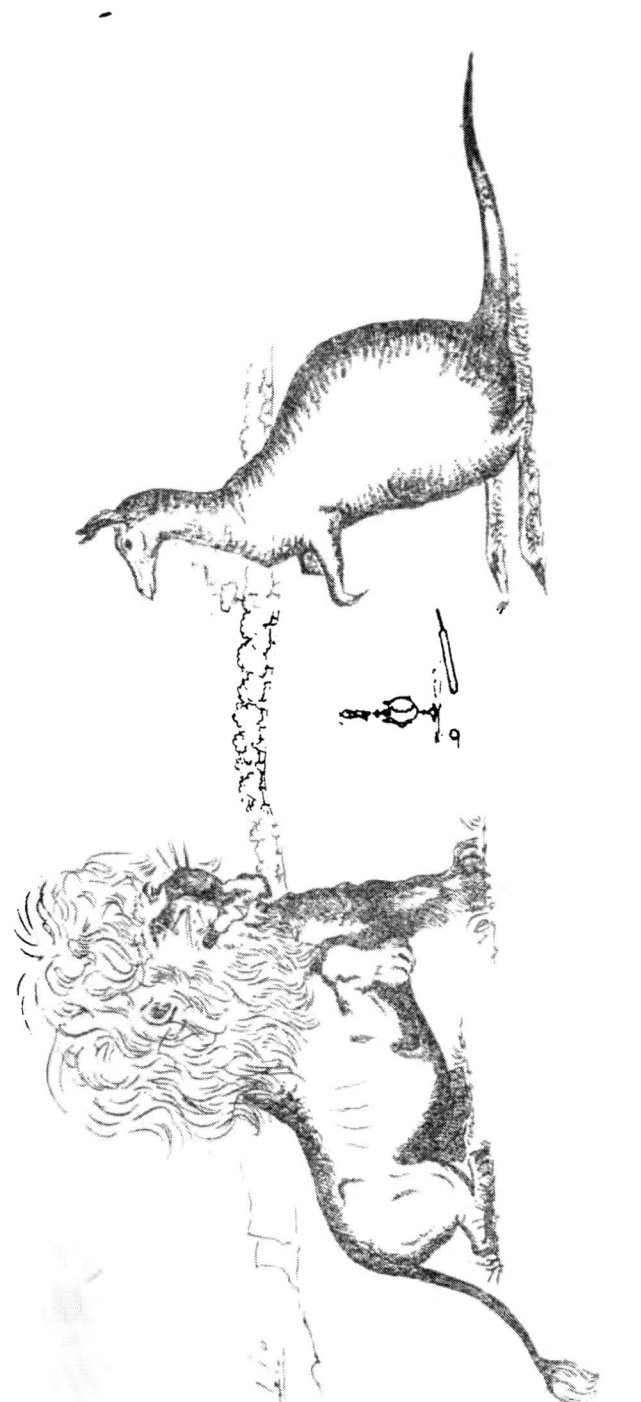

TO BE OR NOT TO BE

BATTING AVERAGES IN MATCHES AGAINST ODDS.

Batsman's Name.	Matches.	Innings.	Times not out.	Most in an innings.	Most in a match.	Total.	Average.
W. W. Read	10	11	1	84	84	338	33·8
E. F. S. Tylecote	10	10	2	59	59	223	27·7
C. T. Studd	10	9	...	99	99	227	25·2
G. B. Studd	8	9	1	45	45	192	24·0
G. F. Vernon	10	10	2	41	41	166	20·6
Hon. Ivo Bligh	6	7	...	45	45	138	19·5
C. F. H. Leslie	10	10	2	51	51	174	19·3
Bates	10	11	2	41	41	161	17·8
A. G. Steel	10	11	3	30*	51	134	16·6
Barnes	10	10	1	42	42	142	15·7
Barlow	10	11	...	39	39	167	15·2
Morley	4	4	1	3	3	5	1·2

* Signifies not out.

BOWLING AVERAGES IN MATCHES AGAINST ODDS.

Bowler's Name.	Balls.	Runs.	Maidens.	Wickets.	Average.
Morley	552	134	80	28	4·22
A. G. Steel	2180	602	259	125	4·102
Barnes	614	168	75	33	5.3
C. T. Studd	1035	30	109	49	6·7
Bates	1163	275	164	35	7·30
G. F. Vernon	20	10	2	1	10.5
Barlow	672	132	109	13	10·2
W. W. Read	184	64	18	5	12·4
C. F. H. Leslie	20	10	2	...	...

BATTING AVERAGES IN ALL MATCHES.

Batsman's Name.	Matches.	Innings.	Not Out.	Most in an innings.	Most in a match.	Total Runs.	Average.
A. G. Steel	17	22	4	135*	156	549	30·9
W. W. Read	17	22	1	84	87	629	29·20
C. F. H. Leslie	17	21	2	144	144	484	25·9
C. T. Studd	17	20	0	99	99	480	24·0
Bates	17	22	3	48*	57	432	22·14
E. F. S. Tylecote	17	21	2	66	71	422	22·14
Barlow	17	23	2	80	80	448	21·7
G. F. Vernon	14	16	3	41	41	226	17·5
Barnes	17	21	2	42	42	258	13·8
Hon. Ivo Bligh	11	16	1	45	45	202	18·7
G. B. Studd	15	21	3	45	45	232	12·16
Morley	9	11	7	3	3	14	3·2

* Signifies not out.

BOWLING AVERAGES IN ALL MATCHES.

Bowler's Name.	Balls.	Runs.	Maidens.	Wickets.	Average.
A. G. Steel	3314	1003	372	150	6·103
C. T. Studd	1813	475	227	58	8·11
Morley	1300	331	185	36	9·7
G. F. Vernon	20	10	2	1	10·0
Barnes	1412	474	150	45	10.24
Bates	2411	704	314	59	11·5
W. W. Read	386	155	36	10	15·5
C. F. H. Leslie	192	67	21	4	16·3
Barlow	2176	605	312	36	16·29

Morley bowled 2 no-balls, W. W. Read 4 no-balls, C. F. H. Leslie 7 wides, and Barlow 1 wide.

FULL SCORE AND ANALYSIS

Of the rival teams at the following matches, as given in the *Melbourne Sportsman* :—

1882.—ON THE MELBOURNE CLUB GROUND, NOVEMBER 17TH, 18TH, AND 20TH.

ALL ENGLAND ELEVEN V. VICTORIA.

ALL ENGLAND ELEVEN.—FIRST INNINGS.

Barlow, 3, 1, 1, 1, 1, 1, 1, 1, 3, 1, 1, 1, 1, 2, 1, 2, 1, 2, 2, 1, 1, 2, 1, 1, 1, 1, 1, 3, 1, 1, 2, b W. H. Cooper 44
C. B. Studd, 1, b W. H. Cooper 1
Bates, 1, 2, 3, 1, 2, 3, 4, 1, 1, 1, 2, 4, 4, 1, 4, 2, 2, 2, 1, 1, 4, 1, 1, c Swift, b M'Shane 48
C. T. Studd, 4, 2, 1, 2, 1, 3, 1, 1, 1, 1, 1, 2, 1, 2, 2, 1, 1, 1, 4, 1, 1, 1, 1, 1, 2, 1, 1, 1, 4, 1, 2, 1, 4, 1, b M'Shane 56
A. G. Steele, 2, b W. H. Cooper 2
W. W. Reed, 1, b J. D. Edwards 1
Barnes, 1, c and b W. H. Cooper 1
E. F. S. Tylecote, 1, 4, 1, 3, 1, 1, 1, 1, 1, 4, 1, 1, 2, 1, 2, 3. 4, 1, 3, 1, st Turner, b W. H. Cooper 37
G. F. H. Leslie, 3, 1, 4, 1, 1, 2, 1, 1, 8, 3, 4, 1, 1, 4. 1, 1, 2, 2, 2, 4, 3, 4, 1, not out 51
G. F. Vernon, 1, 1, 4, 1, 1, 1, 4, 2, 1, 1, b Scott 17
Morley, 2, 1, b Bruce 3
Byes 10
Leg Byes 2

Total... 273

Bowling Analysis.—Cooper, 140 balls, 89 runs, 9 maidens, 5 wickets; Edwards, 112 balls, 39 runs, 12 maidens, 1 wicket; Bruce, 62 balls, 42 runs, 1 maiden, 1 wicket; Scott, 44 balls, 21 runs, 4 maidens, 1 wicket; M'Shane, 100 balls, 37 runs, 12 maidens, 2 wickets; Logan, 48 balls, 48 runs, 2 maidens.

VICTORIA.—First Innings.

J. Swift, 1, 1, 2, 1, 1, 1, 1, c Barnes, b A. G. Steel	8
H. Scott, run out	0
J. D. Edwards, 3, lbw, b Steel	3
J. Rosser, 2, 2, 1, 1, 2, 1, 1, 1, 1, 1, 1, 1, 2, 4, 1, 1, 1, 1, b Read	22
E. Turner, 1, 1, 1, 4, 1, 1, 1, 1, 1, 1. 1, 2, 1, 4, 1. 1, 1, 1, b Read	25
F. Baker, 2, 1, 1, 1, c Tylecote, b Read	5
T. J. D. Kelly, 2, 4, 1, 2, 1, 1, 2, 2, 2, 1, 1, 1, run out	20
W. Bruce, 1, 1, b Read	2
P. G. M'Shane, 2, 1, 3, 1, 1, 2, 1, 1, 2 b Bates	14
W. H. Cooper, b Steel	0
Logan, 2, not out	2
Bye, 1 ; leg-bye, 1 ; no-ball, 1	3
Total...	104

Bowling Analysis.—A. G. Steel, 104 balls, 15 runs, 15 maidens, 3 wickets ; Barnes, 76 balls, 32 runs, 4 maidens ; Bates, 65 balls, 14 runs, 8 maidens, 1 wicket ; W. W. Read, 48 balls, 28 runs, 3 maidens, 1 no-ball, 4 wickets ; C. T. Studd, 44 balls, 6 runs, 6 maidens ; Barlow, 44 balls, 6 runs, 8 maidens.

Second Innings.

H. Scott, 1, 2, 4. 1, 2, 3, 2, 4, 4, b Barnes	26
T. J. D. Kelly, 4, 4, 1, 1, 1, 3, c Leslie, b Barlow	14
J. D. Edwards, 1, 1, b Barlow	2
J. Swift, 3, 2, 4, 3, 1, 1, 1, 2, 1, hw, b Steel	18
J. Rosser, 2, 2, 1, 1, 1, 2, 2, b Steel	11
E. Turner, 2, 4, 1, 4, 1, 4, 1, b Steel	17
F. Baker, 2, 3, b Bates	5
P. G. M'Shane, 4, 2, 1, 1, 1, 4, 2, c Alexander (sub.), b Bates...	15
W. Bruce. 2, 2, 2, 1, 1, 1, 1, 2, 1, 1, 2, 1, 2, 4, 2, 4, 4, 1, 3, 2, 1, c G. B. Studd, b C. T. Studd	40
Cooper, 1, 1, 2, 3, 1, c Tylecote, b Barlow	8
Logan, not out	0
Sundries	13
Total	169

Bowling Analysis.—A. G. Steel, 84 balls, 54 runs, 4 maidens, 3 wickets ; Barlow, 64 balls, 31 runs, 7 maidens, 3 wickets ; C. T. Studd, 93 balls, 19 runs, 16 maidens, 1 wicket ; Bates, 80 balls, 27 runs, 10 maidens, 2 wickets ; Barnes, 48 balls, 19 runs, 4 maidens, 1 wicket ; Read, 16 balls, 6 runs.

Won by England, 4 runs, 10 wickets.

1882–1883.—ON THE MELBOURNE GROUND, DECEMBER 30th, JANUARY 1st and 2nd.

ALL ENGLAND ELEVEN V. AUSTRALIAN ELEVEN.

AUSTRALIAN ELEVEN.—First Innings.

Bannerman, 1, 3, 2, 4, 1, 2, 2, 2, 2, 1, 4, 1, 1, 4, st Tylecote, b Leslie	30
Massie, 4, c and b C. T. Studd	4
Murdoch, 2, 3, 3, 3, 1, 1, 1, 4, 1, 1, 1, 2, 3, 4, 2, 1, 1, 2, 1, 1, 1, 1, 4, 4, b Leslie	48
Horan, c Barlow, b Leslie	0
M'Donnell, 2, 4, 4. 1, 1, 2, 1, 1, 2, 1, 3, 4, 1, 2, 1, 1, 1, 1, 1, 1, 1, 1, 4, 1. b Leslie	43
Giffen, 1, 4, 1, 1, 1, 4, 1, 1, 1, 4, 1, 1, 4, 1, 4, st Tylecote, b Steel	36
Bonnor, 1, 2, 2, 1, 2, 4, 5, 1, 5, 5, 2, 2, 2, 2, 2, 1, 5, 1, 2, 1, 3, 2, 1, 2, 4, 1, 3, 1, 1, 1, 3, 2. 1, 4, 4, 4, c Barlow, b Barnes	85

AUSTRALIAN ELEVEN.—First Innings (continued).

Blackham, 2, 2, 1, 1, 1, 2, 4, 2, 1, 2, 4, 1, 2, c Tylecote, b Studd ... 25
Spofforth, 1, 1, 1, 2, 2, 2, c Steel, b Barnes 9
Garrett, c C. T. Studd, b Steel 0
Palmer, not out 0
Sundries 11

Total 291

Bowling Analysis.—C. Studd, 184 balls, 35 runs, 30 maidens, 2 wickets; Barnes, 120 balls, 51 runs, 11 maidens, 2 wickets; A. G. Steel, 132 balls, 68 runs, 16 maidens, 2 wickets; Read, 32 balls, 27 runs, 2 maidens, 3 no balls; Barlow, 80 balls, 37 runs, 6 maidens, 1 wide; Bates, 84 balls, 31 runs, 7 maidens, 1 wicket; Leslie, 44 balls, 31 runs, 1 maiden, 3 wickets.

ALL ENGLAND ELEVEN.—First Innings.

Hon. Ivo Bligh, b Palmer 0
Barlow, 1, 1, 1, 1, 2, 1, 1, 1, 1, st Blackham, b Palmer 10
Leslie, 2, 2, c Garrett, b Palmer 4
C. T. Studd, b Spofforth 0
A. G. Steel, 3, 4, 2, 4, 1, 4, 1. 4, 4, b Palmer 27
Read, 1, 2, 3, 1, 2, 2, 1, 2, 4, 1, b Palmer 19
Bates, 2, 1, 2, 1, 1, 2, 1, 1, 1, 4, 1, 1, 1, 1, 5, 2, 1, c Bannerman, b Garrett ... 28
Tylecote, 1, 2, 1, 3, 1, 1, 4, 1, 1, 3, 1, 1, 4, 1, 1, 4, 2, 1, b Palmer ... 33
G. B. Studd, 2, 1, 4, run out 7
Barnes, 1, 1, 2, 2, 1, 2, 4, 1, 1, 1, 1, 1, 1, 3, 2, 1, b Palmer ... 26
Vernon, 2, 1, 2, 3, 3, not out 11
Sundries 12

Total 177

Bowling Analysis.—Spofforth, 112 balls, 56 runs, 11 maidens, 1 wicket; Palmer, 210 balls, 65 runs, 25 maidens, 7 wickets, 3 no-balls; Garrett, 108 balls, 44 runs, 6 maidens, 1 wicket.

Second Innings.

Barlow, 4, 3, 1, 3, 1, 1, 1, 1, 1, 2, 2, 1, 2, 1, 1, 1, 1, 1, b Spofforth ... 28
Tylecote, 1, 2, 1, 2, 2, 1, 1, 1, 1, 3, 4, 2, 2, 4, 2, 1, 1, 1, 1, 2, 3, b Spofforth ... 38
C. T. Studd, 2, 4, 2, 1, 1, 1, 1, 2, 2, 1, 1, 3, b Palmer ... 21
A. G. Steel, 1, 1, 1, 1, 4, 2, 4, 4, 4, 1, 1, 2, 1. 1, 1, lbw, b Giffen ... 29
Hon. Ivo Bligh, 1, 1, 1, b Spofforth 3
W. W. Read, 1, 1, 1, 4, 1, 4, 4, 1, 1, 2, 2, 4, 1, 1, 1, 1, b Giffen ... 29
C. H. F. Leslie, 2, 2, b Giffen 4
Bates, 1, 1, 4, 2, 1, 2, c Massie, b Palmer 11
G. B. Studd, c Palmer, b Giffen 0
Barnes, 2, not out 2
Vernon, 3, lbw, b Palmer 3
Sundries 1

Total 169

Bowling Analysis.—Palmer, 145 balls, 61 runs, 11 maidens, 3 wickets, 1 no-ball; Spofforth, 164 balls, 65 runs, 15 maidens, 3 wickets; Giffen, 80 balls, 38 runs, 5 maidens, 4 wickets; Garrett, 8 balls, 4 runs, 1 maiden.

AUSTRALIAN ELEVEN.—Second Innings.

Bannerman, 1, 1, 2, 3, 4, 2, 4, 4, 4, not out 25
Massie, c and b Barnes 0
Murdoch, 3. 1, 2, 1, 2, 2, 3, 2, 3, 2, 2, 1, 4, 2, 1, 2, not out ... 32

One wicket for 57

Bowling Analysis.—C. T. Studd, 56 balls, 17 runs, 4 maidens; Barnes, 52 balls, 6 runs, 8 maidens, 1 wicket; Steel, 36 balls, 17 runs, 4 maidens; Bates, 53 balls, 22 runs, 7 maidens; Barlow, 16 balls, 6 runs, 2 maidens.

Won by Australia by nine wickets.

BEATEN BUT NOT DISGRACED
VICTORIA VICTRIX
12. March 1865.

ON THE MELBOURNE GROUND, JANUARY 19TH, 20TH, AND 22ND.

ALL ENGLAND ELEVEN V. AUSTRALIAN ELEVEN.

ENGLISH ELEVEN.—FIRST INNINGS.

Barlow, 1, 2, 2, 4, 1, 1, 1, 2, b Palmer	14
C. T. Studd, 1, 2, 2, 1, 3, 4, 1, b Palmer	14
C. H. F. Leslie, 1, 3, 3, 2, 3, 1, 2, 3, 3, 3, 2, 2, 3, 4. 1, 3, 2, 1, 1, 1, 4, 2, 1, 3, run out	54
A. G. Steel, 1, 1, 1, 1, 1, 3, 1, 1. 1, 1, 1, 1, 1, 2, 2, 1, 1, 1, 1, 3, 2, 1, 2, 4, 1, 2, 1, c M'Donnell, b Giffen	39
W. W. Read, 2, 1, 1, 1, 1, 1, 1, 2, 4, 1, 4, 1, 4, 2, 1, 2, 1, 4, 1, 1, 1, 4, 1, 1, 2, 1, 1, 1, 1, 1, 1, 4, 1, 1, 2, 2, 4, 2, 4, 1, 2, 1, 3, c and b Palmer	75
Barnes, 4, 1, 1, 1, 2, 1, 3, 1, 4, 4, 1, 4, 2, 1, 2, b Giffen	32
E. F. S. Tylecote, b Giffen	0
Hon. Ivo Bligh, b Giffen	0
Bates, 1, 1, 4, 4, 2, 2, 2, 1, 1, 1, 3, 2, 2, 2, 2, 4, 1, 1, 1, 1, 1, 1, 3, 1, 1, 1, 1, 3, 4, 1, c Horan, b Palmer	55
G. B. Studd, 1, b Palmer	1
Morley, not out	0
Sundries	10
Total	294

Bowling Analysis.—Giffen, 196 balls, 89 runs, 13 maidens, 4 wickets; Palmer, 267 balls, 103 runs, 25 maidens, 5 wickets, 3 no-balls; Spofforth, 136 balls, 57 runs, 11 maidens, 1 no-ball; Garrett, 136 balls, 35 runs, 16 maidens.

AUSTRALIAN ELEVEN.—FIRST INNINGS.

Massie, 4, 4, 4, 4, 1, 2, 3, 4, 4, 2, 2, 1, 4, 1, 1, 1, 1, b Barlow	43
Bannerman, 1, 1, 1, 2, 1, 1, 1, 3, 1, 2, b Bates	14
Murdoch, 1, 1, 1, 2, 1, 1, 2, 4, 1, 1, 1, 1, 1, 1, not out	19
Horan, 3, c and b Barnes	3
M'Donnell, 3, b Bates	3
Giffen, c and b Bates	0
Bonnor, c Read, b Bates	0
Blackham, 1, 1, 1, 2, b Barnes	5
Garrett, 1, 5, 3, 1, b Bates	10
Palmer, 4, 1, 2, b Bates	7
Spofforth, b Bates	0
Sundries	10
Total	114

Bowling Analysis.—Bates, 106 balls, 28 runs, 14 maidens, 7 wickets; Barnes, 92 balls, 32 runs, 7 maidens, 2 wickets; Morley, 92 balls, 13 runs, 16 maidens; 1 no-ball; C. T. Studd, 16 balls, 22 runs, 1 maiden; Barlow, 88 balls, 9 runs, 18 maidens, 1 wicket.

SECOND INNINGS.

Bannerman, 2, 2, 1, 3, 4, c Bligh, b Bates	6
Murdoch, 3, 1, 3, 4, 2, 4, b Bates	17
Blackham, 1, 1, 1, 3, b Barlow	6
Bonnor, 1, 4, 5, 3, 5, 1, 5, 2, 1, 3, 4, c Morley, b Barlow	34
Horan, 3, 1, 4, 2, 1, c Morley, b Bates	11
M'Donnell, 2, 1, 1, 1, 1, 1, 4, 1, 1, b Bates	13
Massie, 3, 1, 4, 2, c C. T. Studd, b Barlow	10
Giffen, 1, 1, 3, 4, 1, 3, 1, 4, c Bligh, b Bates	19

AUSTRALIAN ELEVEN.—SECOND INNINGS (continued).

Garrett, 1, 2, 1, 2, c Barnes, b Bates	...	...	...	6
Palmer, 4, c G. B. Studd, b Bates	...	...	...	4
Spofforth, 4, 2, 4, 4, not out	...	...	...	14
Leg bye	...	...	...	1
Total	...	...	...	153

Bowling Analysis.—Bates, 132 balls, 19 maidens, 74 runs, 7 wickets; Barlow, 124 balls, 7 maidens, 67 runs, 3 wickets; Morley, 8 balls, 7 runs; Barnes, 12 balls, 1 maiden, 4 runs.

Won by England by one innings and 27 runs.

ON THE SYDNEY GROUND, JANUARY 26TH, 27TH AND 29TH.

ALL ENGLAND ELEVEN V. AUSTRALIAN ELEVEN.

ENGLISH ELEVEN.—FIRST INNINGS.

Barlow, 2, 2, 1, 4, 1, 1, 1, 2, 1, 1, 2, 1, 2, 2, 4, c Murdoch, b Spofforth ... 28
C. T. Studd, 1, 4, 2, 1, 2, 1, 1, 1, 2, 1, 1, 1, 2, 1, c Blackham, b Spofforth ... 21
C. F. H. Leslie, b Spofforth 0
A. G. Steel, 1, 3, 1, 4, 1, 1, 2, 4, b Garrett 17
W. W. Read, 1, 2, 1, 2, 3, 4, 1, 4, 2, 1, 1, 2, 4, 4, 1, 4, 1, 1, 4, 3, 1, 4, 2, 4,
    2, 4, 2, c Massie, b Bannerman 66
Barnes, 2, c Blackham, b Spofforth 2
E. F. S. Tylecote, 3, 1, 1, 4, 4, 1, 1, 1, 1, 1, 3, 1, 4, 2, 3, 4. 3, 1, 1, 1, 2, 1, 2,
    4, 2, 4, 4, 2, 1, 2, 1, run out 66
Bates, 2, 2, 1, 1, 4, 1, 2, 1. 1, 1, 1, c M'Donnell, b Spofforth ... 17
G. B. Studd, 1, 1, 1, b Palmer 3
Hon. Ivo Bligh, 1, 1, 1, 3, 2, 1, 1, 3, b Palmer 13
Morley, 2, not out 2
Sundries 12
Total 247

Bowling Analysis.—Giffen, 48 balls, 37 runs, 3 maidens; Palmer, 152 balls, 38 runs, 21 maidens, 1 no ball, 2 wickets; Spofforth, 204 balls, 72 runs, 19 maidens, 5 wickets; Garrett, 108 balls, 54 runs, 8 maidens, 2 wickets; Bannerman, 44 balls, 1 wicket; M'Donnell, 24 balls, 16 runs.

SECOND INNINGS.

C. F. H, Leslie, 4, 3, 1, b Spofforth 8
C. T. Studd, 2, 1, 2, 4, 2, 1, 3, 1, 2, 4, 3, b Spofforth 25
Barlow, 1, 4, 1, 2, 4, 4, 1, 1, 1. 1, 1, 3, c Palmer, b Horan ... 24
A. G. Steel, 2, 2, 2, lbw, b Spofforth 6
W. W. Read, 2, 1, 1, 4, 1, 4, 1, 3, 4, b Horan 21
Barnes, 1, 2, lbw, b Spofforth 3
H. F. S. Tylecote, c Bonnor, b Spofforth 0
Bates, 1, 2, 1, c Murdoch, b Horan 4
Hon. Ivo Bligh, 1, 3, 2, 2, 1, 4, 4. not out 17
G. B. Studd, 4, 1, 3, 1, c Garrett, b Spofforth 8
Morley, b Spofforth 0
Sundries 7
Total 123

Bowling Analysis.—Spofforth, 165 balls. 44 runs, 23 maidens, 7 wickets; Garrett, 53 balls, 31 runs, 3 maidens; Palmer, 36 balls, 19 runs, 3 maidens; Horan, 68 balls, 22 runs, 10 maidens, 3 wickets.

AUSTRALIAN ELEVEN.—First Innings.

A. C. Bannerman, 1, 4, 1, 1, 4, 1, 1, 4, 4, 1, 4, 1, 3, 4, 4, 1, 2, 4, 2, 1, 4, 2, 3, 2, 1, 1, 4, 1, 1, 3, 1, 1, 1, 4, 1, 2, 2, 4, 4, 2, c Bates, b Morley ... 94
G. Giffen, 1, 1, 2, 1, 1, 1, 1, 2, 1, 4, 4, 1, 1, 2, 1, 1, 1, 3, 2, 1, 4, 2, 2, 1, st Tylecote, b Bates ... 41
W. L. Murdoch, 1, 1, 1, 2, 2, 2, 3, 1, 1, 2, 1, 1. 1, lbw, b Steel ... 19
P. M'Donnell, b Steel ... 0
T. Horan, 2, 1, 1, 1, 1, 1, 2, 1, 4, 1, 2, 1, 1, c Steel, b Morley ... 19
H. H. Massie, 1, c Bligh, b Steel ... 1
G. Bonnor, c G. B. Studd, b Morley ... 0
J. Blackham, 1, 1, 4, 1, 1, 1, 3, 2, 1, 4, 2, 2, 2, 1, 1, b Barlow ... 27
T. Garrett, c Barlow, b Morley ... 0
G. Palmer, 2, 1, 1, 3, c G. B. Studd, b Barnes ... 7
F. Spofforth, not out ... 0
Sundries ... 10

Total ... 218

Bowling Analysis.—Bates, 180 balls, 55 runs, 20 maidens, 1 wicket; Morley, 136 balls, 47 runs, 16 maidens, 4 wickets; A. G. Steel, 104 balls, 27 runs, 14 maidens, 3 wickets; Barnes, 52 balls, 22 runs, 6 maidens, 1 wicket; C. T. Studd, 56 balls, 5 runs, 11 maidens; Barlow, 189 balls, 52 runs, 31 maidens, 1 wicket.

Second Innings.

Giffen, 1, 4, 2, b Barlow ... 7
Bannerman, 4, 1, c Bligh, b Barlow ... 5
Murdoch, c G. B. Studd, b Morley ... 0
Horan, 4, 1, 1, 1, 1, run out ... 8
M'Donnell, c Bligh, b Morley ... 0
Massie, 2, 4, 4, 1, c C. T. Studd, b Barlow ... 11
Bonnor, 1, 1, 2, 3, 1, b Barlow ... 8
Blackham, 1, 1, 2, 2, 4, 3, 2, 1, 2, 4, 1, 3, b Barlow ... 26
Spofforth, 1, 2, 1, 2, 1, c Steel, b Barlow ... 7
Palmer, 2, not out ... 2
Garrett, b Barlow ... 0
Sundries ... 9

Total ... 83

Bowling Analysis.—Morley, 140 balls, 34 runs, 10 maidens, 2 wickets; Barlow, 138 balls, 40 runs, 20 maidens, 7 wickets, 1 wide.

Won by England by 69 runs.

ON THE SYDNEY ASSOCIATION GROUND, FEBRUARY 17TH, 19TH, 20TH AND 22ND.

ALL ENGLAND ELEVEN V. COMBINED AUSTRALIAN ELEVEN.

ENGLISH ELEVEN.—First Innings.

Barlow, 2, c Murdoch, b Midwinter ... 2
C. T. Studd, 2, 2, 2, 1, 4, 1, 1, 1, 3, 2, 1, 1, 1, 1, 4, 1, 1, 3, 2, 4, 2, 2, 3, 1, 1, 1, run out ... 48
C. F. H. Leslie, 2, 4, 2, 1, 1, 3, 3, 1, c Bonnor, b Boyle ... 17
A. G. Steel, 2, 1, 1, 2, 4, 1, 1, 4, 2, 1, 1, 4, 2, 3, 4, 4, 1, 1, 3, 2, 1, 4, 2, 1, 1, 1, 4, 3, 1, 1, 4, 2, 2, 1, 4, 1, 1, 1, 1, 4, 3, 4, 2, 1, 2, 1, 1, 1, 2, 1, 2, 2, 1, 1, 1, 1, 1, 4, 3, 4, 4, 4, 1, not out ... 135

W. W. Read, 1, 1, 3, 1, 4, 1, c Bonnor, b Boyle 11
E. F. S. Tylecote, 4, 1, b Boyle 5
Barnes, 2, b Spofforth 2
Bates, 2, 1, 1, 1, 1, 1, 1, 1, c Bonnor, b Midwinter 9
Hon. Ivo Bligh, 1, 1, 4, 4, 3, 2, 4, b Palmer 19
G. B. Studd, 3, run out 3
Morley, b Palmer 0
    Byes, 4 ; leg-byes, 7 ; no-ball, 1 12
                                                              —
    Total... 263

Bowilng Analysis.—Palmer, 96 balls, 52 runs, 9 maidens, 2 wickets, 1 no-ball ; Spofforth, 34 balls, 56 runs, 8 maidens, 1 wicket; Midwinter, 188 ball, 50 runs, 24 maidens, 2 wickets ; Boyle, 160 balls, 52 runs, 19 maidens, 3 wickets ; Horan 48 balls, 26 runs, 4 maidens ; Evans, 44 balls, 15 runs, 3 maidens.

AUSTRALIAN ELEVEN.—First Innings.

Bannerman, 1, 3, 4, 2, c Barlow, b Morley 10
Bonnor, 2, 3, 2, 1, 2, 2, 1, 2, 2, 1, 2, 3, 1, 2, 4, 1, 2, 3, 4, 2, 2, 2, 4, 1, 4, 4, 1,
  4, 1, 2, 2, 2, 2, 1, 4, 3, 3, 2, c Barlow, b Steel 87
Murdoch, b Barlow 0
Horan, 2, 1, 1, c G. B. Studd, b Morley 4
Giffen, 4, 4, 2, 1, 4, 4, 2, 2, 3, 1, c G. B. Studd, b Leslie 27
Midwinter, 2, 4, 3, 1, b Barlow 10
Blackham, 1, 3, 2, 1, 1, 4, 3, 4, 1, 4, 1, 1, 3, 2, 1, 3, 3, 2, 1, 2, 4, 2, 4, 4, b
  Bates 57
Palmer, c Bligh, b Steel 0
Evans, 2, 4, 2, 1, 1, 3, 2, 1, 1, 1, 1, 1, 1, 1, not out 22
Spofforth, 1, c Bates, b Steel 1
Boyle, 1, 1, 4, 1, 3, 2, 1, 1, 3, 3, 1, 3, 2, 3, c G. B. Studd, b Barlow ... 29
Sundries 15
                                       —
    Total 262

Bowling Analysis.—Barlow, 192 balls, 88 runs, 21 maidens, 3 wickets ; Morley, 176 balls, 45 runs, 25 maidens, 2 wickets; Barnes, 40 balls, 33 runs, 2 maidens ; Bates, 60 balls, 24 runs, 6 maidens, 1 wicket ; Leslie, 20 balls, 11 runs, 2 maidens, 2 wides, 1 wicket ; Steel, 72 balls, 34 runs, 6 maidens, 3 wickets ; C. T. Studd, 24 balls, 12 runs, 2 maidens.

ENGLISH ELEVEN.—Second Innings.

Barlow, 2, 1, 1, 1, 2, 1, 2, 1, 2, 1, 1, 1, 2, 1, 1, c Bonnor, b Midwinter ... 20
C. T. Studd, 1, 1, 4, 1, 4, 1, 1, 2, 1, 4, 3, 1, 2, 1, 1, 3, c Murdoch, b Midwinter 31
C. F. H. Leslie, 2, 2, 2, 1, 4, 2, 2, 4, b Horan 19
A. G. Steel, 1, 1, 4, 2, 3, 1, 1, 1, 1, 1, 1, 1, 1, 2, b Spofforth 21
W. W. Read, 2, 1, 1, 1, 2, b Spofforth 7
E. F. S. Tylecote, b Palmer 0
Bates, 1, 1, 4, 1, 1, 3, 1, 4, 2, 1, 1, 2, 1, 2, 2, 1, 2, 2, 2, 1, 4, 1, 1, 3, 1, 2, 1, not out 48
Hon. Ivo Bligh, 3, 1, 4, 1, 1, c Murdoch, b Horan 10
Barnes, 2, 4, 2, 1, 2, 1, 3, 2, 1, 1, 1, c and b Boyle 20
G. B. Studd, 3, 1, 3, 2, c Murdoch, b Boyle 9
Morley, 2, c Blackham, b Palmer 2
Sundries 10
                                      —
    Total 197

Bowling Analysis.—Spofforth, 112 balls, 57 runs, 6 maidens, 2 wickets ; Boyle, 92 balls, 35 runs, 6 maidens, 2 wickets ; Palmer, 175 balls, 59 runs, 19 maidens, 2 wickets ; Midwinter, 92 balls, 21 runs, 13 maidens, 2 wickets ; Horan, 36 balls, 15 runs, 2 maidens, 2 wickets.

THE BURIAL OF THE ASHES.
MIDNIGHT
13 MARCH 1883.

AUSTRALIAN ELEVEN.—Second Innings.

Bannerman, 2, 4, 1, 2, 1, 1, 1, 1, 1, 2, 2, 1, 1, 1, 1, 3, 4, 4, 3, 2, 1, 3, 5, 4, 4, 4, 3, 1, c Bligh, b C. T. Studd,	63
Murdoch, 1, 2, 1, 4, 2, 2, 1, 2, 1, 1, c Barlow, b Bates	17
Bonnor, 3 c G. B. Studd, b Steel	3
Horan, c and b Bates	0
Giffen, 4, 3, 4, 1, 1, 2, 1, 2, 2, 1, 2, 1, 1, 1, 1, 1, 1, 2, st Tylecote, b Steel	32
Blackham, 1, 3, 1, 1, 3, 2, 1, 1, 1, 1, 2, 2, 1, 4, 2, 4, 1, 2, 1, 1, 1, 1, 4, 3, 1, 3, 1, 2, 3, 4, not out	58
Evans, c Leslie, b Steel	0
Midwinter, 1, 2. 2, 1, 2, not out	8
Byes, 10 ; leg-byes, 4 ; wides, 4	18
Total for six wickets	199

Bowling Analysis.—Bates, 156 balls, 52 runs, 19 maidens, 2 wickets; Barlow, 149 balls, 44 runs, 20 maidens; Steel, 172 balls, 49 runs, 10 maidens, 3 wickets; Morley, 36 balls, 9 runs; Leslie, 32 balls, 23 runs, 4 wides; C. T. Studd, 32 balls, 8 runs, 4 maidens, 1 wicket; Barnes, 64 balls, 22 runs, 5 maidens.

Won by Australia by 4 wickets.

ON THE MELBOURNE GROUND, MARCH 12TH.

ALL ENGLAND ELEVEN V. VICTORIA.

VICTORIAN ELEVEN.

M'Donnell, 3, 3, c Bates, b Barnes	6
Blackham, 1, run out	1
Bonnor, 2, 4, 1, 1, 1, 1, 2, 1, 2, 1, 1, 1, 1, 1, 4, 1, 2, 4, 1, 4, 4, 5, 2, 2, 1, 1, 2, c Tylecote, b Barnes	54
Scott, 3, 2, 3, 2, 1, 4, 4, 1, 3, 1, 2, 2, 1, c Tylecote, b Barlow	29
Horan, 2, 1, 2, 2, 1, 3, 3, 3, 1, 1, 2, 1, 1, 1, 1, 2, 4, 1, 2, 2, 1, b Barnes	37
Midwinter, 2, 2, 1, 2, 1, 1, 1, 2, 1, 1, 1, 4, 1, 1, 1, 3, 1, 1, 1, 1, 1, 2, 4, 4, 2, 4, 1, 2, 4, 4, 1, 1, 4, 1, 1, 2, 1, 1, 2, 1, 2, 1, 1, 3, 3, 1, 1, 1, 1, 1, 4, not out	92
Palmer, 1, 1, c Steel, b Barnes	2
Turner, 1, 4, 4, 1, 4, 1, 1, 1, 1, c Barlow, b Steel	18
Boyle, 1, 1, 2, c Tylecote, b Steel	4
M'Shane. 4, 1, 1, 1. 3, 3, 1, 3, 2, 1, 1, 1, 4, 1, b Bates	27
Cooper, 1, lbw, b Barnes	1
Sundries	13
Total	284

Bowling Analysis.—Barnes, 206 balls, 70 runs, 23 maidens, 5 wickets; Steel, 220 balls, 79 runs, 25 maidens, 2 wickets; Bates, 148 balls, 52 runs, 21 maidens, 1 wicket; Barlow, 100 balls, 34 runs, 11 maidens, 1 wicket; C. T. Studd, 104 balls, 13 runs, 16 maidens; Read, 24 balls, 6 runs, 3 maidens; Leslie, 76 balls, 17 runs, 9 maidens.

ALL ENGLAND ELEVEN.

First Innings.

E. F. S. Tylecote, 3, 1, b Cooper	4
C. T. Studd, 1, 2, 1, 1, 4, 1, 1, b Cooper	11
Bates, b Palmer	0
C. F. H. Leslie, lbw, b Palmer	0

A. G. Steel, 2, 4, 4, 1, b Cooper 11
W. W. Read, 1, 1, 2, 1. 1, 1, c Midwinter, b Cooper 7
Barlow, 1, 1, 2 not out 4
Barnes, 3, 1, 1, 1, 4, 1, run out 11
G. F. Vernon, 1, 2, b Boyle 3
G. B. Studd, 1, 1, b Palmer 2
Ivo Bligh, b Palmer 0
    Sundries 2

    Total 55

SECOND INNINGS.

Barlow, 2, 1, 1, 1, 1, 1, 1, 1, 1, 1, 1, 3, 1, 1, 1, 4, 1, 1, 1, 2, c M'Donnell, b Palmer 27
C. T. Studd, 2, 1, c Blackham, b Palmer 3
Bates, 1, 1, 1, 1, 1. 1, 1, 1, 2, 2, 1, 2, 2, 1, 1, 1, 1, b Palmer 21
C. F. H. Leslie, 1, 2, 1, 3, 2, c Horan, b Midwinter 9
A. G. Steel, 1, 1. 2, 1, 1, 1, 3, 4, 2, 1, 3, 4, 2, 1, 3, 2, 4, 1, 1, 1, 1, 2, 1, 2, 1, 4, 1,
  2, 1, 1, 2, 1, 2, 4, 2, 2, 2, 1, 1, 3, b Palmer 76
W. W. Read, 4, 1, 1, 3, b Palmer 9
E. F. S. Tylecote, b Palmer 0
Barnes, 2, c Blackham, b Turner 2
G. F. Vernon, 2, c and b Palmer 2
G. B. Studd, not out 0
Ivo Bligh, st Blackham, b Turner 2
    Sundries 5

    Total 156

Bowling Analysis.—Cooper, 52 balls, 29 runs, 5 maidens, 4 wickets, 1 no-ball; Palmer, 61 balls, 21 runs, 6 maidens, 4 wickets; Boyle, 12 balls, 3 runs, 1 maiden, 1 wicket. Second Innings.—Boyle, 84 balls, 29 runs, 7 maidens; Palmer, 192 balls, 65 runs, 19 maidens, 7 wickets; Midwinter, 60 balls, 17 runs, 5 maidens, 1 wicket; M'Shane, 16 balls, 8 runs, 2 maidens: Turner, 36 balls, 18 runs, 1 maiden, 2 wickets; Horan, 12 balls, 3 runs, 2 maidens; Cooper, 36 balls, 11 runs, 3 maidens 1 no-ball.

Won by Victoria by one nnings and 73 runs.

"WHAT WILL THEY SAY IN ENGLAND"

EH, IVO! OH, IVO! [ASK PUNCH.]

W. MUDDIMAN

MANUFACTURER

AND

IMPORTER

13 WELL STREET,

FALCON SQUARE,

LONDON, E.C.

Manufactures of all kinds pushed throughout the Colonies. Advertisements Received for all Australian Papers at 20 per cent. less than London Agents.

Albert S. Manders & Co.

MELBOURNE, ADELAIDE. SYDNEY & LONDON.

THE AUSTRALIAN

Manufacturers' and Commission Agency.

IMPORTANT NOTICE.

FIRST CLASS

AGENCIES WANTED

FOR THE

AUSTRALIAN COLONIES.

The undersigned are prepared to accept Agencies, and will work them in the Colonies of Victoria, New South Wales, and South Australia, and advertise the same free.

ALBERT S. MANDERS & CO.

Head Office: 91 Little Collins Street E., Melbourne, Victoria.

LONDON REFERENCES.

LONDON REPRESENTATIVE:

W. MUDDIMAN, 13 Well's Street, Falcon Square, LONDON, E.C.

Printed by Libri Plureos GmbH in Hamburg, Germany